White
Spells
for
Protection

About the Author

Originally from Cuba, Ileana Abrev now lives in Queensland, Australia, where she has her own spiritual practice and conducts workshops on magic, spirituality, meditation, chakras, and crystals. She has built a reputation for herself as a respected white witch among her customers and clients. With knowledge passed down to her from her father, an esteemed Santero, Ileana guides customers on a daily basis to solve problems with simple magic spells and positive visualization. She has been a practicing witch for over ten years.

White Spells for Protection

Ileana
Abrev

Llewellyn Publications
Woodbury, Minnesota

First Edition
First Printing, 2007

Book design by Steffani Sawyer
Editing by Brett Fechheimer
Cover design by Lisa Novak
Cover art and interior illustrations by Mary Ross
Llewellyn is a registered trademark of Llewellyn Worldwide, Ltd.

Library of Congress Cataloging-in-Publication Data:
Abrev, Ileana, 1959–
  White spells for protection / Ileana Abrev. — 1st ed.
     p. cm.
  Includes index.
  ISBN: 978-0-7387-1085-3
  1. Magic. 2. Charms. I. Title.
  BF1611.A268 2007
  133.4'4—dc22
                                        2007012310

Llewellyn Worldwide does not participate in, endorse, or have any authority or responsibility concerning private business transactions between our authors and the public.
  All mail addressed to the author is forwarded but the publisher cannot, unless specifically instructed by the author, give out an address or phone number.
  Any Internet references contained in this work are current at publication time, but the publisher cannot guarantee that a specific location will continue to be maintained. Please refer to the publisher's website for links to authors' websites and other sources. **Note:** These spells are not to be used in lieu of professional advice.

Llewellyn Publications
A Division of Llewellyn Worldwide, Ltd.
2143 Woodale Drive, Dept. 978-0-7387-1085-3
Woodbury, Minnesota 55125-2989, U.S.A.
www.llewellyn.com

Printed in the United States of America

Also by Ileana Abrev
White Spells

Forthcoming by Ileana Abrev
White Spells for Love

Contents

Dedicated to all who believe in justice

Thank you Mum and Dad for all your help with
White Spells for Protection when we were up on Macona

Introduction

Strike Me Not

Strike me once, strike me twice,
but never shall you strike me
a third time around.

If a total stranger, or even someone you knew, came to your front door and for no reason suddenly slapped you in the face, how would you react? At first, you'd probably be confused about what had just happened. But before you had enough time to react, imagine that you got slapped once again. Now you're no longer shocked and a hidden anger stirs deep within you. You ask yourself, "What have I done to deserve this?" when suddenly you see the hand ready to strike you once again. This time you are aware and ready to protect and defend yourself. This time you reach out and hold the hand before it has time to strike you, saying "Don't you ever hit me again!"

Protection and defense magic works similarly. It kicks in when enough is enough and it's time to start diminishing those negative energies by catching the bullet before it gets you. Protection and defense magic is not about revenge. It's about looking after yourself when others are trying to harm you with magic.

When performing defense magic, you must always take karma into account. The laws of karma should be respected at all times. The universe is well aware of those inflicting physical or emotional harm against innocent souls by means of negative magic. When such an injustice is committed, it is known to the universe—and the perpetrator is paid back threefold.

Unfortunately, we don't know when the universe will justify others' wrongs. The process could take weeks, months, years, or it could even go toward that individual's next lifetime. In the meantime, you sit and wait. While you do, the negative soul gets away with all types of injustices toward you or your loved ones.

You have every right as a member of the universe to protect yourself against these types of people; you don't have to just sit there and take the injustice. Act wisely and use protective and defensive magic.

If you have a problem using this type of magic, think of it as an alarm system for your home to keep intruders from entering and taking what is yours. Remember that such people deserve no pity. They certainly have none for you when they start to use destructive forces.

Never feel guilty when using white spells. We are all human, and it is human instinct to protect our territory from danger and against negative individuals who only want to inflict emotional or physical pain. If your heart is pure, you could never do anything against the laws of karma or against a fellow soul member.

Positive thoughts create loving, healing energies while negative thought patterns can be classified as curses— curses that are potentially very harmful to any individual at whom they're aimed. The funny thing about negative thought patterns is that the people who produce them are sometimes unaware of doing so, which means such negative thoughts are often transmitted very innocently to someone who doesn't deserve them. Yet others are well aware of their negative thought patterns and transmit them very viciously in order to cause harm intentionally.

Such individuals carry with them a negative obsession to destroy whoever they "believe" has done them wrong. Their thought patterns are filled with malice but can only produce destructive energies when directed toward someone else. These people will stop at nothing to destroy you.

Their greed is driven very passionately by their egos in order to manipulate others whom they consider to be weaker. They do this to obtain control and to cause harm and destruction to anyone who gets in the way of their own goals.

Thoughts directed toward anyone in such a negative manner do penetrate the aura field, more so when physical defenses are down due to stress or illness. Such factors can make you even more vulnerable and susceptible to negative thoughts. You become like a sponge, unconsciously absorbing negative thought forms that are hanging over you just waiting to strike you down.

The sad part is that the person sending you all these negative thoughts has no moral conscience and doesn't care about your well-being. Such a person might be disguised as your neighbor, one of your relatives or co-workers, or even your best friend. Always be aware. Your gut feeling never lets you down and you will know who the carrier of negativity is.

Eventually, you'll begin to ask yourself what you've done to this person to make him or her act this way. Well, you may have done absolutely nothing. He or she may not even know what you have done but may nonetheless be filled with an unknown hatred toward you while battling with internal insecurities and jealousy. Such people are carrying a negative obsession against you, which has lodged itself in their corrupted minds, and they will stop at nothing until their negative thoughts result in physical or emotional harm.

During my years of experience helping others to protect and defend themselves against these types of injustices, I have come to the conclusion that people who seek this type of destruction toward another soul are often out to destroy happiness at any cost.

Unfortunately, if they aren't able to accomplish what they set out to do with negative thoughts and actions, frustration sets in and it is at this point that some seek magic to finish the job. You may be asking, "What type of magic?" Well, in the world of magic, there are corruptive forces that I call "the malignant tumors of the occult."

The malignant tumors are not your everyday true practitioners; they are out there practicing destructive magic—that is, if the price is right. These people should not be categorized with those who have personal pride in their magical workings. Everyone who practices true magic is well aware of those who certainly do not.

We have all experienced sadness in life and all of us appreciate laughter when it comes around. Magic is the same way: black or white, positive or negative, you need to have experienced both to know the difference. For example, let's say that you could wish death on a person by lighting twenty black candles, aiming destructive thoughts toward the person. With positive protective and defensive magic, the magic could work in reverse. You could light pink and white candles to wish a person peace within while also asking him or her to leave you alone. There is a difference; it's how you practice magic that makes you a true practitioner, and without that understanding there can never be a balance to the soul.

Sadly, many people have the wrong idea about magic. The Hollywood image has been a damaging one and it is only beginning to change. We witches don't have big noses covered in warts but are beautiful people with intelligence who possess goodness in our hearts. This reality is slowly coming across. Just because magic is practiced does not mean that it is negative, destructive, ugly, or evil.

I am deeply concerned when people approach me to conduct their dirty workings. An example: a few years ago, a lady who had been having an affair with a married man for about six months came to see me. The man had left this woman because he still loved his wife and wanted to make their marriage work. This woman was beside herself and wanted me to break up their marriage so he would go back to her. I tried to reason with this woman for more than an hour but she wouldn't listen to anything I had to say and told me flat out, "If I can't have him, neither can she!" and walked out.

 xxi

I heard through the grapevine a few weeks later that she paid five thousand dollars for someone to do her negative workings. I felt sorry for her, and the person who took her up on it, and sent protective loving energies to the married couple.

Like this woman, hundreds of thousands of people are out there looking for someone to do their negative workings. Once they find this person, they don't ask moral or ethical questions. They only discuss destruction to an innocent soul and the cost involved to start the dark workings, money that is often paid willingly even when the price is a small fortune.

The most common form of black magic practiced is the application and manipulation of essence, when a part of someone—a piece of clothing, a strand of hair, nail clippings, a photograph, or another sort of personal item—is stolen and used. Such an item is taken to the person conducting the negative workings, who now has a piece of the subject's essence and generally uses it to weaken the aura field. This is one of the worst types of manipulative magic as it works against one's own energies, the essence of one's soul.

When the manipulation of essence penetrates the aura field, it may manifest in lack of energy or sleep, a loss of finances, a sudden unexpected illness, disharmony in the home, bad luck, accidents, a feeling of being lost and unloved, hair falling out, or the end of a strong, years-long relationship.

Mental and physical strength is the first ground rule for working against negative forces. If you feel sick, act as if you're on top of the world. If you know that someone is working against your own energies, then it's not the time to seek sympathy from others. This is very important. If the negative source finds out you have been ill, then your defenses are down—and that is when they strike the hardest. The negative source may find out about your illness when someone you know, or the friend of a friend, feeds them the information. It could all be very innocent but, before you know it, the information gets back to the person working against you.

Some of the things that are done are horrific and hard to believe. I have witnessed some of the most sickening and selfish aspects of human nature, and there is no turning back once someone is on that path of destruction.

These people tap into spells that would make your hair stand on end: spells to bring illness to a victim, to separate a man and a woman or to break up a marriage, to attract another against his or her will, or to break a mother's heart by turning her children against her. Or they might invoke curses to give someone an ulcerous tumor, to intentionally harm someone with the use of wax dolls, to destroy a business, to cause fights in the home, to force the loss of a home from lack of finances, to seek vengeance from someone, or to steal others' psychic gifts. Others try out sexual curses to leave a man impotent, to bring bad luck, or to manipulate a lover. Some have even cast a spell to blind or silence a dog.

Now you can understand why protection is needed against these types of spells, which are dangerous to anyone they're aimed at. Imagine if you had no way to fight back against this type of injustice; it would be like a home invasion during which you are helpless to retaliate and your life is at the whim of others who can, at the very least, leave you emotionally scarred forever.

Chapter One

Man and Universal Law: Defense and Protection

1

$\mathcal{I}$t is very important to know how to defend and protect yourself against negative forces. The key to overriding this type of magic is to be aware, to know how to defend yourself, and to know when to do so.

Our own individual upbringings and beliefs as well as the larger society have engraved on our subconscious that taking justice into our own hands is "wrong"—and rightly so. We have no right to take the law into our own hands and to judge others for the wrongs they have done. This is the "human law," the law that keeps the masses under control for the good of society.

But we are also participants in a universal law, to which we all hold a free membership. As acting members of the universe, we all have the right to protect and defend ourselves and our loved ones against any type of injustice, whether it comes from a negative source or the mugger down the street who hits us over the head and takes our money. Just as you would seek justice by taking the mugger to court, so you can do the same with those sending negative thoughts your way.

The human law and the universal law are very similar in many ways. The human law is there to protect us and to defend the innocent; this is also the purpose of the universal law, but with it you have to protect yourself, too. If your home were broken into and you didn't have an alarm system or property insurance, then you'd be at a loss. The law can try to catch the thieves and you would ideally retrieve some of your personal items, but we know very well that doesn't always happen.

After such a robbery, you tell yourself it won't happen to you ever again, so you install an alarm system and buy property insurance. The law can help you, but you also have to help yourself and protect yourself against such an injustice.

The universal law works the same way. As I've already stated, the universe is aware of anyone who inflicts unnecessary physical or emotional harm by means of negative magic. But you still need to protect and defend yourself against any type of negative magical workings.

You have every right to protect and defend yourself against any type of injustice. Think of such protection as an alarm system for your home that will stop intruders from taking what is yours and hurting you and the ones you love.

At some point in our lives, most of us have needed to protect and defend ourselves from a bully of some sort or have defended ourselves against an unfair accusation. Even Disney movies show us how good always confronts and defeats evil, always with magical endings filled with happiness, hope, and everlasting love.

You can fight back if dark occult forces are out to get you. There is always a will and a way, and your will and way will be much stronger than theirs. Yours comes from the heart; theirs is completely filled with hate. I can assure you that karma is on their tails every step of the way—whereas the universe is your knight in shining armor, there to protect you.

Chapter Two

Have You Been Cursed?

Don't always blame magic for your misfortune. There are numerous types of curses that we inflict upon ourselves, and these are very similar to those that come from others.

This is why it is so important to analyze even the smallest hiccup in your life before blaming it on someone else. Remember that we do have the right to defend ourselves, but not to accuse someone unjustly. This is where the hard work starts. You need to ask yourself the following questions:

1. Are you feeling tired or ill for no reason?
2. Do you feel life is not worth living?

3. Is your hair falling out?
4. Is there a personal item missing?
5. Has your financial situation changed in the last three months?
6. Are there more than the usual misunderstandings in your home?
7. Have you lost your job?
8. Are you unable to find work?
9. Have you become accident-prone and had a stream of bad luck?
10. Is your marriage or relationship falling apart for no reason?
11. Are you unable to find love in your life?
12. Is everything you do going wrong for no valid reason?

If you have answered "yes" to about 75 percent of the questions, you could be under some type of negative influence, but we can't just stop there—let's do a bit more detective work. Make a list of friends and family that visit your home or workplace often. Divide the list in two columns, a positive one and a negative one.

After you finish the list, have a look at your negative column and I'll bet you there is a person on that list who visits and leaves you completely without energy. We all have one of those friends. These sorts of friends are called "vampires of light." They will even tell you, "I feel so good when I talk with you." They're harmless; they just need light that they can't produce for themselves because of their own lack of self-esteem, which is why they feed from your own supply, leaving you mentally exhausted.

The next person on the list could be someone from your place of employment—a boss or a co-worker. These people may feel some type of jealousy toward you and wish they had your work abilities, or they might be jealous that you got the promotion they'd wished for. They could willingly be sending negative thought patterns to you, which can become an issue for protection in your place of employment.

Then there is the family friend or family member who you really don't want to have around. This person could be harmless, but there might be a clash of personalities. Or he or she could be someone you've just never particularly gotten along with or liked. You need to judge if this person has gotten over your disagreements, and if they haven't, they need to stop sending all those negative thoughts to you. This issue should be addressed and stopped with protection.

We also have many acquaintances. We talk and have fun with lots of people, but true friends are hard to find. Yet we all generally know at least one person with whom we share our thoughts and feelings, and this person should be treasured. If you've counted more than five close friends, then check your list again and find the friend who always says "I'm there for you"—but actually isn't. This one could be the thorn you have been looking for but never knew existed.

By the same token, this person could be someone who starts rumors and quietly tells your partner something you did, changing the story so that it is very different from what you remember. This person could also be in love with your partner, with thoughts that are no longer friendly toward you; unfortunately, those thoughts could be starting to penetrate your aura field. If there is anything missing from your home and this person was the last one to visit, then there is a good chance he or she is up to no good. In this case, protection is a must—before this person breaks up your home and your relationship by manipulation of essence.

The next person on the list could be someone who taps into occult forces. Just be aware, and make sure they only practice positive magic. You can tell if they do; something about their aura is always clean and welcoming. If you don't feel this, this person could very well be practicing negative magic, especially if they talk of vengeance and payback. If that is the case, stay away. These people are not mature enough to understand that there is spirituality in all magical workings.

Then there are self-inflicted curses that do not necessarily result from negative occult forces. These curses can be broken, and they must be dealt with in order to move forward and find a better understanding. If you're dealing with such a curse, you need to stay positive and work on personal issues or your issues around the other people who are holding you back from your own spiritual growth.

To break any type of curse, you can start by ignoring all negative written material that you come across, including chain letters. These are "seal curses," and they penetrate the subconscious mind. Just ignore them and don't give in to them. If you do give in to them, you will make the curse manifest. It's best to burn the letter and sprinkle salt on top of the ashes. As for chain letters, just throw them away. Remember that if you give in to such a curse, you will make whatever was written happen.

Stay away from people who use "perpetual curses." These curses are inflicted by partners, parents, or others who are close to you and are physically or verbally abusive. People who are constantly telling you that you are worthless and will amount to nothing without them will naturally make you feel timid and scared, and make your natural defense system collapse. They have actually cursed you. This curse is easy to overcome once you take the first step by physically walking away from those who have cursed you and seeking professional aid.

There are other curses—like the "unforgiven curses" that are carried from past lives. You can break these by doing meditations and past-life regressions to find out how you can fix the wrongs of your past life in this lifetime. Other things that you may feel are holding you back —such as, for example, fear or a phobia—also hold back your spiritual and personal growth.

Don't blame others for the "curses within." By not feeling good about yourself, you—and you alone—are responsible for these curses. Believing that you are too fat, too skinny, or "just plain ugly" is a type of curse and you will need to do some positive visualization about yourself to find the truth behind this self-hate within you. This curse can be reversed by programming your subconscious mind into always thinking in a positive way about who you are—a child of the universe with inner beauty that comes straight from the soul.

We should treat our minds like computers. Everything we want, we should keep—and what we don't want, we should trash. But the hard drives in many people's minds are always full. Such people hold on to emotions like hurt and sorrow, and in so doing fill up their hard drives, which then don't allow them to experience new and wonderful things because they are full of trash. Empty your hard drive and transfer that which you wish to forget to a disk so you can always open it if you wish. File the rest in your hard drive and save it as "joy and happiness.doc."

Just remember, if you think you have been cursed, you will be, so stay positive at all times. The more you think about the curse, the more those who have cursed you will be able to intrude on your spiritual space. Don't let them; you are stronger than they are. You have the goodness of the universe on your side, and it will not let any injustice into your sacred space if you are willing to fight back.

Chapter Three

Getting Started

You ou need a place to conduct your magical workings. A bedroom or the living room in your home is fine. The place itself isn't important; just make sure that you can work without being bothered by family members or room- mates. It's always better to do your magical workings alone and in private, unless you specifically want or need some- one else to be there. The reason is very simple: some people don't understand, and they judge without knowledge. Their judgment can be very detrimental to any magical work- ing, and could scatter the energies you wish to send out to the universe. Another's negativity about what you are doing and trying to achieve will affect the direction of your energies, and your thoughts will not reach the desired destination.

Once you have found a place to conduct your magical workings—let's call it your sacred site or altar—you should set up a small table. (A card table is good, as you can fold it up when it's not in use.) There is no right or wrong way to set up your sacred site; just do it according to your tastes, faith, and beliefs.

There are numerous items needed, and energies used, to conduct spells. It's always good to have all the items that you might need at hand, or at least to know what these items are—and to be able to understand why they are used.

Candle holders

Sometimes, you will be using a few candles at the same time, so it's always good to have many candles around. You can purchase inexpensive candle holders—there's no need to go to great expense. Brass candle holders can tarnish and look disagreeable; and if your candle holders look bad, you might not remain focused on your magical workings.

Candles

The colors of candles are very important in any type of magical workings. Each color has a magical meaning and is used to promote and enhance that particular desire. When you purchase a candle, make sure that the candle colors described on the outside of the box are the same as the actual colors of the candles inside. Also, if a spell requires a blue candle, you should ensure that the candle burns all blue—and not white in the middle and blue on the outside.

Candles need to be dressed if you are using them for a magical purpose. For any type of magical intent, the candle is divided into two parts. From the middle of the candle up toward the wick is called the *North Pole*, and from the middle down to the end is the *South Pole*.

When a spell indicates that you should dress the candles, you must rub each candle with the oil specified in the spell. Rub a bit of the oil in both of your hands. Encircle the candle with your right hand and bring that hand from the center of the candle up the North Pole of the candle. Next, encircle the candle with your left hand and bring that hand down from the center of the candle along the South Pole of the candle. Never rub both of your hands simultaneously in an up-and-down motion.

You can dress the candles with olive oil, unless the beginning of the spell specifies differently. Always visualize the task at hand when you are getting the candles ready for magic.

There are also astral-colored candles you will use when a spell requires a candle in a specific person's astral color, according to his or her star sign.

Astral Colors		
Aries	May 21–April 19	White
Taurus	April 20–May 20	Red
Gemini	May 21–June 21	Red
Cancer	June 22–July 22	Green
Leo	July 23–Aug. 22	Red
Virgo	Aug. 23–Sept. 22	Black
Libra	Sept. 23–Oct. 22	Black

Astral Colors (cont.)		
Scorpio	Oct. 23–Nov. 21	Brown
Sagittarius	Nov. 22–Dec. 21	Gold
Capricorn	Dec. 22–Jan.19	Red
Aquarius	Jan. 20–Feb. 18	Blue
Pisces	Feb. 19–March 20	White

Candle snuffer

Candle snuffers are a must. Candles should never be blown out because, in doing so, a spell immediately loses its intent. And let me tell you: it's no fun extinguishing ten candles with your fingers. Invest in a candle snuffer. Believe me, the money will be well spent.

Vase for flowers

A vase is optional. I like to have fresh flowers on my altar at all times, as they keep the room fresh and full of love. It's good to have fresh flowers on your altar, even if just for your daily meditations or positive visualizations.

Mortar, pestle, and herbs

You should have a mortar and pestle to use in your kitchen to blend herbs together. In magic, the mortar and pestle are also used to mix and crush different herbs together to cause a desired effect. Herbs are very important in magic. For example, rosemary leaves are not only for garnishing your lamb roast; in magic, rosemary can also be used for protection, intellect, and love. The best mortars are those made of wood.

Censer and charcoal tablets

You can use a small bowl for your censer, or a tiny cauldron with three legs; it doesn't matter if it's made of metal or glass. You can burn dry herbs on their own by lighting a match to them. Or to get more out of your dry herbs or resins, just fill the bottom of the censer with either dirt or sand—even rock salt—to insulate the container, then place a charcoal tablet on top. It's better to light it outside the house as it initially gives off a not-so-pleasing gray smoke. Then, when it becomes red hot, you can add your herbs on top of the charcoal. Be aware that the charcoal tablets are a fire hazard and should be treated with care. Do not drop them on the floor or use them around small children—the burns are very painful.

Oil burner and essential oils

An oil burner is not just used in aromatherapy for medicinal purposes or to alleviate stress. Essential oils are often used in magical workings as well, and their strength is concentrated to focus on an intent or to dress candles for magic. Oil burners are usually ceramic, and you should choose one based on your own individual tastes. You may even already have one in your cupboard.

The pentagram

The pentagram is a five-pointed star used at times for protection, and while working with and representing the elements.

Elements

In some of the spells, you will utilize elemental forces for strength and wisdom to aid with the spell. The elemental forces are earth, water, air, and fire. The elements are embedded deep within the soul of every single one of us. They keep us in touch with the self and function in unison with each other to calm the storms in our hearts, and to help us to grow spiritually, to make the right choices, and to have the firepower to fight for what we believe is right.

Earth (green)

Earth is the grounding force of our needs. It allows us to accept what we have until we reach our desired goal.

Water (blue)

The emotions are controlled by this element. It puts us in touch with past hurts in order to transform that pain into knowledge. It can wash away the deepest hate, and turn it into love and understanding. But most of all, the water element shows us how to forgive.

Air (yellow)

Air lights the light that is deep in all of us. It strengthens our ideas to make them realities. It is the air that we breathe. Without air, we cease to exist.

Fire (red)

The fire element is the driving force behind making everything that we need or want come to be. The fire element gives us strength and reason to fight for what we believe and that which we wish to achieve.

Color

Color is an essential part of any type of magical workings and should be used whenever possible to enhance that need.

Follow the chart on the next two pages and use color to promote peace, health, happiness, wealth, and protection. You can also wear a color to enhance any actual spell. In doing so, you will be showing the universe what you need.

Color	Meaning
Amber	Develops psychic abilities and communication with spirits and guides. Provides a deeper meditation state.
Black	Wards away negativity, removes hexes, protects against evil workings, and promotes truth in magic.
Blue	Brings peace and tranquility, banishes anger, gives protection against others' negativity and unwelcome thought patterns.
Gold	Strengthens the mind. Can be used in money spells and in communicating with the higher realm.
Green	Luck, used for money and self development spells. Heals emotional pain. Helps spiritual growth.
Purple	For third-eye workings and meditation.

Color	Meaning
Lavender	Peace, spiritual development, and restful sleep.
Orange	Encouragement, fertility spells.
Pink	Attracts friendship, brings love within to be able to love others and be loved in return.
Red	Strength, power, protection, and courage needed to fight against negative forces.
White	Peace and purity, protection for children and your home. Brings justice, and helps you to work and communicate with your spiritual guide.
Yellow	Understanding, communicating with others, and learning. Sparks the intuition and warns against dangerous situations.

Chakras

The chakras are the healing life force in our bodies and the source of our survival. Chakras can be used in magic to protect or enhance a particular life point. There are seven main chakras; beginning at the base of the spine and finishing at the top of the head, they are:

Root (red)
Located at the base of the spine.

Abdominal (orange)
Located in the lower abdomen.

Solar plexus (yellow)
Located under the breastbone.

Heart (green)
Located at the center of the chest.

Throat (blue)
Located at the center of the throat.

Third eye (purple)
Located in the center of the brow.

Crown chakra (pink)
Located above the head.

Crystals

Crystals also play a big part in magic and are an excellent tool to use with your spells. There are hundreds of crystals out there. If you are unable to identify one, just visit your nearest lapidary association; they will be more than happy to find or identify what you need or have. When crystals are worn, they amplify the etheric body and in turn strengthen your aura field by acting as a coat of steel to protect your sacred space. Crystals need to be cleansed before being used, even if a particular spell does not specify cleansing. The best way to cleanse a crystal is to place it in a mixture of water and a teaspoon of salt. Leave the bowl containing the crystal, salt, and water in your backyard or on your front porch for three days and three nights, after which your crystal will be ready to use and program.

Calendar with lunar phases

Most calendars note lunar phases; make sure your calendar does so as well. The phases of the moon are frequently used in magical workings. When the moon is full or new, you can do any type of magical working. You should perform positive spells when the moon begins to wax (increase), and when the moon starts to wane (decrease), you will want to perform spells to get rid of negativity, bad influences, negative workings, and even your own negative energies.

Meanings of days of the week, planets, and colors

Each day of the week has a meaning; if you do a spell on a specific day of the week, using the assistance of the planets to guide you and help direct your intent, you will be totally focused and will work in conjunction with the forces of the universe.

Day	Planet	Color	Meaning
Sunday	Sun	Yellow	Protection, healing the self and illness, money spells
Monday	Moon	White	Psychic abilities
Tuesday	Mars	Red	Courage, leadership, strength
Wednesday	Mercury	Purple	Communication
Thursday	Jupiter	Blue	Money, legal problems, and personal goals
Friday	Venus	Pink	Love, relationships
Saturday	Saturn	Black	To get rid of opposing negative forces

Now you are ready to start! It is very important to include your positive attitude and visualization to any of the spells you do, as well as to add all the tools already mentioned. Visualizing your needs to the universe is a required part of any magical work. The more you visualize, the stronger the possibility is that the intended desire will reach its destination. Don't confuse protection or defense with manipulation of others; if you do, you will need to answer to karma. Always remember that what goes around comes back around.

Chapter Four

Tools for Protection

Protection tools chart

The chart on the following two pages will help you identify days of the week, crystals, colors, herbs, and candles for quick reference when you are conducting spells or when you need protection.

Protection Tools Chart			
Day of the week	Monday	Tuesday	Wednesday
Candles	Black	Blue	White
Herb	Basil	Frankincense	Myrrh
Colors	Black	Blue	White
Crystal	Apache tears	Tiger-eye	Carnelian
Protection	Protection for finances	Strength to fight against negative forces	Communication to solve altercations with negative people

Protection Tools Chart (cont.)			
Thursday	Friday	Saturday	Sunday
Red	Blue and red	White and black	Yellow and black
Garlic	Dragon's blood	Rice	Rosemary
Red	Blue and red	White and black	Yellow and gold
Ruby	Red jasper	Aquamarine	Agate
Strengthen spirituality against negative forces	Protection against someone taking away a loved one	Fighting against negative forces	Protection against illness

Chart for getting rid of negativity

This chart can be used when you are in a hurry and don't have the time to do an actual spell. As long as you maintain positive visualization, you can accomplish your needs quickly and easily with this chart.

Bad spirits	Light a black candle and a white candle and burn frankincense in the house on Saturdays and repeat again on Tuesdays.
Negative energies	To stop negative energies in their tracks, write down on a piece of paper the negativity you wish to end, stick it in a glass of water, and freeze it.
Evil	In your censer, burn frankincense together with dragon's blood in the morning and at night to clear all types of evil.
Gossip	Write on a red cloth the name of the person who is spreading gossip, then fold the cloth and tape it together. Bury it under a dying plant and the gossip will end soon enough.

Un-hexing	Add a tablespoon of salt, half a cup of coconut milk, half a teaspoon of olive oil, and a teaspoon of dry rue to a warm bath. Bathe in this mixture for seven nights.
Protection for the home	Keep a few old keys in a bowl behind the front door; then make an arrow out of cardboard. Write the protection needed by your home on the arrow and place it on top of the bowl facing the front door to keep anyone with bad intentions out of your home.
Protection for young children	Have young children carry or wear a tiger-eye crystal and they will be protected.
Protection of finances	Burn green candles in your place of employment and always have fresh basil around.

Negative magic	Keep an apache tear crystal or a little red ribbon with you at all times to protect you or your loved ones from any negative workings. Wear black for protection, or wear red for strength against negative occult forces to reinforce your etheric body. You can also wear a pentagram pendant or visualize one over your chest every morning before you leave the house.

Chapter Five

Once, Twice, but
Not a Third Time Around

have deliberately divided up the spells in this book to suit the "strike me once, strike me twice, but never shall you strike me a third time around" method. This division will help you gauge the severity of your needs and deal with them accordingly, as there are things that can be fixed with simple spells and not lengthy rituals.

Strike me once—the warning: be aware

The "strike me once" method is a quick-fix spell to ward away negative energies. This method could cover anyone from your boss giving you a hard time to the mother-in-law who never shuts up. It can also be used on entities and occult negative forces around you and in your home that you wish to expel. The strike me once method stops negative energies in mid-air. Like ice, they become frozen in time until they slowly fall to the ground without any direction or intent. It also serves as a warning signal for those sending negative energies that you are aware of their negative intentions.

Strike me twice—the second warning: be prepared

The "strike me twice" method should be used when you feel your first warning has failed. The message in strike me twice is to say "One more time and you're out!" This method will have a little bit more firepower and more tools will be used, such as candles or crystals.

Never a third time—the third warning: act upon it

This method is the final action. "Never a third time around" is used when the first two actions have failed, and people have suffered emotional or physical pain from negative forces like negative thought patterns or occult forces.

You will use the "third time around" action when there are hexes to be broken and curses to undo. This action is to be used only for when you have had enough of being the nice guy and you must stop the injustice aimed at you or your loved ones.

Long gone are the days when you needed to actually see someone to break a hex or help you with defensive magic. You can do it all yourself better than anyone else could. The key is to follow the rituals or the warning spells and to stay totally positive. Never say to yourself, "Did it work?" Instead, tell yourself, "It worked! I can feel it!" The spells are only there to keep you focused with the aid of natural energies that will manifest your needs. Your positive visualization sends these energies out into the universe with a bang, and you will never look back.

Stay focused, search your heart, and above all, make sure you are on the right track. Never blame the innocent—get your facts right before you do any of these spells; if uncertain, you can always do a protection spell with no names attached to it. In this way, the universe will find the person doing you wrong and direct the spell toward that person, ensuring that it's delivered to the one who is not in tune with the forces of nature.

Chapter Six

Spells for the "Strike Me Once" Method—
The Warning: Be Aware

Blue Light of Protection

Visualize a blue light around your home and family every morning. Doing so will protect your home from those who are sending negativity to your home.

Knots of Love

Tie seven knots on a piece of rope. Then, dress a pink candle with lavender essential oil and the piece of rope. Light the candle and visualize peace to the one who wants war, and he or she will leave you alone.

Hairy and Ugly

If you keep a coconut behind your front door, no one can harm you with negative actions or thoughts.

Lock Them Up

A key tied with a blue bow behind the door will lock away unwelcome energies that are penetrating your home.

Triangle Trap

Fill three glasses with water, and then make sure they touch each other in a triangle formation. Place them where no one can touch them in order to protect your home from negative entities.

Not to Be Seen

Wear a pair of red underpants inside-out to keep away the negative energies sent from people who wish to destroy your sex life.

Baby Be Safe

Place a tiger-eye and an apache tear crystal in a little blue bag and hang it inside your baby's crib or stroller to keep your baby safe and sound.

Unforeseen Events

Don't find yourself unprotected from uncontrollable situations. Tie a blue, red, and white ribbon together and carry it with you at all times.

Stinky and Sticky

Burn raw brown sugar on a charcoal tablet after unwanted visitors leave your home. This will be good for the well-being of your home.

Four Corners

Fill four bottle caps with household ammonia and place them in the four corners of your home. Doing so will keep your home safe and secure.

Gossip

Use a pin to write on a black candle the name of the person who is spreading harmful gossip. Place the candle in the freezer and the gossip will cease.

Absorb It

Before you go to bed at night, leave a glass of water where your family gets together to sit down, talk, and relax. In the morning when you wake up, take the glass outside and throw its contents onto your front lawn. All the negative energies from the day before will be absorbed into the water and will be gone.

Chakra Protection

Get a meter (about three feet) each of red, orange, yellow, green, blue, purple, and pink ribbons. Make a braid out of the ribbons, then tie the braid around your waist to strength your chakras, so no one can mess with or weaken them.

Right Foot Forward

Every morning, leave the house with your right foot first. In doing so, no one can take away your right of way.

Vamp Zap

Hang a bunch of garlic from your front door to keep away unwanted negative forces from your home. Don't use the garlic for cooking—that's not what it's there for!

Reflection

Always have a mirror facing your front door—it will reflect those negative thoughts from unwanted visitors back where they came from.

Blue Pen

Tie a blue ribbon around the pen you use in order to protect your space from those who wish to ridicule your work.

Clear Quartz

Wear a clear quartz crystal to repel negative forces from penetrating your aura field.

Angry Boss No More

Sweeten up your boss by writing his or her name on a piece of paper and then pouring honey all over it. Leave the paper alone for a few days and you will see the change take place. Repeat again whenever needed.

Peace and Quiet

Light blue and white candles whenever you need to keep your home a peaceful haven.

Another Four-Corner Job

Get four clear quartz-point crystals and place them in the four corners of your home for protection against the forces outside your control.

Protection Smoke

Burn frankincense incense on Saturdays to keep your home clean from negative forces. Doing so will give such forces no choice but to get up and go.

Howdy, Neighbor

For a neighbor to be friendlier, mix dry thyme and white sugar in a bowl and sprinkle the mixture between both your homes. This will help you to get along better.

Oh, Not the Mother-in-Law!

Light a pink candle and, before your mother-in-law arrives, recite out loud: *"See no mess; smell no shame; the children are okay; there is no need to speculate because you love us anyway."*

A Thorn at Work

Mix together half a teaspoon of cumin powder and one teaspoon of dry angelica, and sprinkle them around the person's work station. Visualize this person getting along with others or finding another job.

Flick Away

When you feel you have picked up negative vibes from someone, flick a white hanky all around you. The negative energies you picked up will go away as quickly as they came.

Protection with Crystals

No matter the crystal's shape or size, carry one with you at all times just in case—and you will forever be protected.

Light Zappers

As soon as you know that this person is coming, rub a little bit of frankincense essential oil in your hands. When this person enters your home, give them a big hug or a pat on the back. Doing so will prevent them from taking your energy away with them.

I Wish You to Leave

Place a straw broom behind the front door with a touch of salt on the top. This will make the unwanted visitor think about their own home—and they will quickly leave yours.

Entities Begone

Place as many garlic peels as you can on top of a charcoal tablet. The resulting smell will make any entities go away. (You can do the same with sulfur, but don't inhale; it's toxic!)

Hate Gossip?

Sprinkle salt around you and no gossip will ever come near you.

Rosemary

Wear a small branch of rosemary close to your heart and no emotional upset will enter your heart from others who wish you harm.

Sweet Protection

Make a pentagram out of large or small cinnamon sticks, using copper wire to keep it all together. Hang the pentagram behind your front door and sweet protection will forever be in your home.

Evil, Eat Your Heart Out

Carry dill seeds in a little red drawstring bag to keep evil people away.

Fresh as Pine

If one isn't already there, plant a pine tree outside your front door. It will protect your home all day while you are at work.

Theft Control

Place three old keys in a little red drawstring bag. Fill the bag with caraway seeds, and hang it above the front door. It will prevent people from taking what is yours.

Bundle of Protection

Tie three acorns together with a red ribbon and hang them outside your front door for protection from any negative forces wanting to invade your peaceful home.

Spirits Begone

Place a teaspoon of dry boneset and a tiger-eye crystal inside a little blue drawstring bag. Carry it with you for protection against evil spirits.

The Bogeyman

Place caraway seeds in a little dream pillow to protect the young from nightmares and from being scared.

Circle in the Middle

Make a small circle with pinecones, and in the middle place a teaspoon of asafetida. Draw a pentagram with your fingers on top. Doing so will protect you from negative occult forces.

Chapter Seven

Spells for the "Strike Me Twice" Method— The Second Warning: Be Prepared

To Stop an Altercation with Neighbors

Light a yellow candle and burn benzoin essential oil in your oil burner. Fill a basket with ripe peaches. As you place each peach in the basket, visualize you and your neighbor actually being nice to each other. The next morning, leave the basket of peaches at the neighbor's front door and sneak back to your home. From that moment on, you will get a kind morning greeting and a smile from next door or across the road.

Protection for an Innocent Soul

Mix a teaspoon of olive oil and half a teaspoon of dill seeds together on a Saturday, while thinking of the one that you seek protection for. Rub the mixture on a blue candle and embed as many dill seeds as you can into the candle. Write the name of the person you seek protection for on a piece of paper and place it under the candle—and then light the candle for about ten minutes. Light the same candle for ten minutes every day for seven days, always visualizing this person and wishing them no harm.

Astral Protection

Before astral traveling, light a white candle and ask your guide to direct and protect you against any harm in the astral world. Always hold a fresh clipping of rue, and then begin your travels with peace in mind. You will come to no harm from the ones who want to try and harm you.

Bad Luck out the Door

Light a white candle on a Saturday morning. While the candle burns, start cleaning your home. Use ammonia to clean the floors, and sprinkle rock salt over any carpeting. After all is clean and tidy, burn hawthorn berry, dry basil leaves, and two or three frankincense tears in your censer. Diffuse this smoke all over the house to leave good energies behind and to get rid of all the bad luck. Vacuum up the rock salt before noon on the following day.

Not My Child, You Don't!

When your child leaves for school, open his or her bedroom window. Light one yellow candle and one red candle in the room. Doing so will give your child strength. Burn hyssop and sage together in your censer and take this sacred smoke into the room to help your child deal with peer pressure. Let the candles burn for a while and let the smoke linger so that the protection your child needs will keep.

Envy Me Not

Mix together a teaspoon of castor oil with seven pepper-corns as you visualize the person who envies you so much. Dress a candle with the oil and embed the seven pepper-corns within the candle. As you watch the candle being consumed, the person's envy will melt away, never to cause you pain again.

Clearing the Self

Take the following items into your bathroom: a white candle, your censer with the charcoal already lit to burn, three frankincense tears (open the window as it will be very smoky), two white flowers, and an egg that has been out of the fridge for about an hour. Undress in privacy and place the censer on the floor by your feet. Pass the flowers all over your body, and do not stop until all the petals have landed on the floor. Open your arms and let the smoke engulf you, close your eyes, and visualize the wrongs leaving your soul and feel all the negativity others have placed on you as gone. Then hold the egg above your head and visualize it absorbing all the negativity in and around you. Next, run the egg all over your body—think of it as soap being used on a dry body. When you finish, crack the egg and flush it down the toilet. (Don't flush the eggshells though!)

Salt and Pepper

Draw a warm bath and add to the water one tablespoon of salt, a quarter teaspoon of black pepper, and a generous amount of dry rosemary. Light a white candle and a black candle and sit back and enjoy this magical bath. Make sure you wet your hair, as this bath will get rid of negative energies that have been sent purposely toward you. It will revitalize your aura and make your spirits high, ready to soar to the sky while negative energies become a thing of the past.

Not My Partner

Burn a rose incense stick and light a pink candle. While you do so, visualize your spouse or partner and how much you are in love with each other. Bring to mind the person trying to take your partner away from you, and place an imaginary stamp on this person's forehead and in your mind mail her or him all the way to Japan. Now visualize this person staying away from the one you love. Hold an Adam and Eve root and a carnelian crystal in your hand. Run them over the smoke from the incense and candle, thinking only of the one you love staying home. Place both the crystal and the root in a little red drawstring bag and place it under your partner's pillow. The lady or man friend who is after your partner will soon be packing up and going away.

Repel Evil Away

Place a block of camphor, a teaspoon of dry angelica, and some valerian and basil leaves in a kitchen pot you no longer use. Add four cups of water and bring the mixture to a boil. Carry your steaming pot around the house while chanting: *"Repel, repel evil away, never to be felt again."* You can do this whenever you feel the need to clear space.

Chili Peppers to Go, Please!

Buy a dozen large chili peppers on a Tuesday (or even better, use homegrown ones if possible). Rub castor oil on each and every one of the peppers, making sure you wash your hands after doing so. You need a large blue cloth. A sheet also works well, as the fabric has to cover you up. Go out into the night, sit in your yard, and make a circle around you with the chili peppers. Then throw the blue cloth over yourself, visualizing all the evil gone and protection for your soul.

Protect Your Business

Make a cross out of two red pencils. Then light four green candles around the pencils and sprinkle Irish moss, yerba santa, and onion peels on top. Visualize the protection you seek for your business and from the one who wants you in the red. Do this on a Sunday and let the candles burn for about an hour.

Take Hatred Away from the One Who Hates

Make a heart-shaped pocket out of a red cotton cloth and place the name of the person who hates you inside it. Mix together rose petals, lemon peels, and catnip, and then add a few drops of vanilla essence. Stuff this mixture inside the heart-shaped pocket and sew the opening up. Light a pink candle while you visualize the hate leaving this person's heart, to be replaced with joy and happiness. Do this on a Wednesday and the hate will be gone.

Stop in the Name of Love

If someone is trying to take away the person you love, write the name of your loved one on a large piece of paper. Place some witch hazel and raw brown sugar on top of the name and wrap it all up. Tie the package with a red ribbon and place it under the bed of the one you love—this will keep the hands of the octopus away!

Peace

As long as there is peace in the home, negative energies will not penetrate, since these energies require discord and arguments to feed from. If there is tension in your home, burn a few cooking cloves and fresh rosemary leaves on a charcoal tablet. You can do this anytime you want to keep your home at peace.

Only at My Front Door

To keep negative entities from entering your home, light a white candle outside your front door. Negative entities need light to grow and develop spiritually. A lit candle at your front doorstep helps the entities "get it," and they will see no need to come in to have a feast.

Up to No Good

Light a pink candle and a blue candle in the center of your altar while visualizing the negative force from which you need protection. Place a carnelian agate and an apache tear crystal in a black drawstring bag; then also place a High

John the Conqueror root inside this little protection bag. Light a frankincense incense stick, run the bag over the smoke, and make a wish for all those up to no good to be gone, never to harm you as long as you carry this bag close to your heart. You can do this for anyone in need.

Super Banger

Mix a half-teaspoon of blessed thistle, angelica, dragon's blood, frankincense, and myrrh together in your mortar and pestle. As you crush them together, visualize the entity you wish gone. Light a white candle and a blue candle; then start what I call the "Super Banger": burning the herbs together in your censer for maximum protection against negative entities in your home. Bring this smoke all over the house and chant: "Go, go, begone and never return!"

Wash Away

Unfortunately, after you have a bad day at work, you can't help but bring into your home all the negative energies that have stuck to your aura field. When this happens, draw a warm bath and light a white candle in the bathroom. Add an entire tablespoon of vinegar, a cup of milk, and a cup of pineapple juice to the bath. Stay in this bath for about ten minutes and visualize all the worries of the day washing away. When you take out the plug, watch your bad day go down the drain.

Prison Dirt

Sweep the dust and dirt from a prison's front door and take it home. Place the dirt in a little blue drawstring bag and make a note on parchment paper: "You will never harm me, because in prison you will be—the iron bars stopping you from ever harming me." Put this note in the drawstring bag and keep it with you at all times.

Light of Protection

Half an hour before you go to work in the morning, light a blue candle and visualize the protection needed by your family and home. Then visualize the ones you love inside the candle's flame with a blue protection light around them. No one will ever harm them or intend to harm them, as the light of justice is on your side.

Get Rid of the Ugly Past to Make the Future Bright

Get rid of the wrongs imposed by others' evil eyes. Go back to the first time bad luck started to follow you around. Remember the date and write it down with a pin on a black candle. Now add a dash and write down the date on which you're conducting the spell. On a green candle, write the date of the spell with the same pin, followed once again by a dash, and then write the year 2099. Light the black candle first and visualize it consuming and melting all the wrongs you wish to rid yourself of, and then light the green candle. Visualize all that you wish to accomplish in this lifetime, with only good luck from the date of this spell until 2099. Both candles must consume all the way to the end. The spell will then start working for the end of bad luck and for good luck to come your way.

Abuse Not My Hospitality

If someone visits every day at a certain time and stays too long, write their name on a piece of parchment paper along with the following: "When you come to visit, please don't stay long. You are needed in your own home." Fold the paper nice and tight and place it inside a toy vehicle that looks like the car your visitor drives or the bus he or she takes to get to your home. Place the toy car or bus close to your front door ready to drive away.

The Death Card

Light two blue candles on your altar and place the Death card from a tarot deck between the candles. Place an anise star on top of the card and then sit back and visualize the end of what is bothering you or the person you wish to stop bothering you. See the mysterious horseman on the Death card moving across your troubled path and taking with him everything that interferes in your life. Let the candles burn down halfway, and then relight them the next day until they reach their end. Discard the anise star in a place where there will never be any growth, but will see rebirth.

Psychic Protection Pot

Place a cup of water, a teaspoon of blue food dye, one teaspoon of wood betony, and a carnelian agate crystal inside an old pot that you no longer cook with. Bring all this to a boil. When it steams, carry it all over the house. Doing so will protect you from unexpected psychic attacks and sudden negative energies that could make the hairs on the back of your neck stand on end.

Let's Get Along Better Together

Would you like to make amends and improve a situation for everyone's sake? Sprinkle coriander around the person you want to get along with—you can even sprinkle it on the person's front door—and you will start to get along better. With business rivals, rub your hands with coriander before shaking their hands—and you will have a better understanding of each other's business and what your rivals want.

For Unstable Minds

Mix crushed dry rosemary leaves with two drops of marjoram oil until a paste is made. Then rub the whole mixture on a pink candle. Write on the candle the name of the person who is unknowingly causing harm to everyone with whom he or she makes contact and whose negative energies you want to stabilize. Patience is required as these people suffer from mental illness. They do not consciously mean you harm, but both protection and awareness are needed in order to understand them.

Chapter Eight

Spells for the "Never a Third Time Around" Method—
The Third Warning: Act Upon It

To Remove a Curse

This spell will remove curses placed before your time by ancestors. You can also use it for more recent curses and for friends who have been cursed for someone's self gain. You can also do this ritual to exorcise unwanted entities from a corporal being.

You will need:

- Eggshell of 1 egg
- 2 blue candles (dress with castor oil)
- 1 black candle (dress with castor oil)
- 1 barbecue charcoal
- Censer and a charcoal tablet

- 1 teaspoon of angelica

- 1 teaspoon of blessed thistle

Method:

Crack an egg and empty its contents; then place the shell on top of a white piece of paper and leave it in the sunlight to dry. Once dry, crush the eggshell in your mortar and pestle, making it into a powder. As you do this, keep the curse you wish to terminate in your mind.

On a Tuesday when the moon is waning, light the two blue candles and visualize what you wish to be gone. Then light the black candle while visualizing the hurt this curse has caused. See the curse being consumed by the flame of the candle. Place the black candle between the blue candles.

With the barbecue charcoal, draw a pentagram on your forehead and a pentagram on your chest, visualizing the pentagrams drawing out the curse that was placed upon your physical and spiritual self.

Mix the angelica and the blessed thistle and start burning the mixture in your censer. Next, anoint your forehead and chest with the powder of the crushed eggshell. As you do so, say:

"Evil that was placed upon me shall no longer exist.
YOU will terminate this day and leave this sacred site,
my body, and my life."

Stop for a moment and focus completely on the words you are speaking. See all the wrongdoing leave your body like a suction cup; when you feel it leave, say with strength:

"STAY AWAY . . . BE GONE
for the good of my soul and all!"

With the eggshell powder, draw a circle around the black candle and then quickly extinguish the candle with your right index finger. Follow this by immediately breaking the black candle in half, visualizing all that was done to you breaking apart in front of your eyes. Take the candle and bury it deep in a place where you know it will never surface again. From this date forward, you will be your old self again.

Protection Using the Chakras

Using the chakras, you can protect against both enemies and negative energies that want to emotionally or physically weaken you and those you love. This is an excellent spell to use for individuals who have been physically or verbally abused. It should give such people the strength they need to make the abuse stop. If you are using this spell for such a purpose, visualize the abused person's needs and see her or him as you go through each chakra in the spell. Place the abused person's name under the white candle.

You will need:

- 1 white candle (dress with marjoram essential oil)
- 1 of each of the following candles: red, orange, yellow, green, blue, purple, pink (dress with corn oil)
- A bunch of eucalyptus leaves
- 1 teaspoon of fennel
- 1 teaspoon of sage
- 7 sunflower seeds
- 1 meter (about three feet) of red ribbon
- 1 small piece of paper

Method:

Mix the fennel and the sage together in your mortar and pestle on a Sunday when the moon is either full or nearly full; then burn the mixture in your censer one bit at a time. Light the white candle and visualize the one from whom you are defending yourself. Write your name, or the name of the person you are helping, on the piece of paper and place it under the candle. Then light all the other candles. Each color represents one of your chakras and its representative color, and you must therefore visualize what each color represents as follows:

- *Red:* Visualize the root chakra, the center of your emotions, stronger than ever before.

- *Orange:* Visualize the abdominal chakra nursing lovingly your relationships with loved ones, making those relationships strong and bonding.

- *Yellow:* Visualize the solar plexus, your gut feeling, never being wrong.

- *Green:* Visualize the heart chakra, your heart center,

strong with all past issues resolved.

- *Purple:* Visualize the third eye, your psychic powers, expanding so you can see who is doing your soul wrong.
- *Pink:* Visualize the crown chakra, your spirituality, growing and understanding the faults of others.

Visualize a rainbow with these colors around you. See them like swirls never breaking the circle. Once all the candles are lit, put them into a circle with the white candle in the middle. Visualize the white candle's flame engulfing your etheric field and the gold wings of angels lovingly around you. Say:

> *"From those who wish me harm*
> *I will be* [or: *You will be*] *forever protected.*
> *I have the gold wings of angels on my side*
> *And they embrace me with protection*
> *Fight me not, for it is you the*
> *Golden army will be after."*

Sprinkle the sunflower seeds and the eucalyptus leaves in the center of the circle. Visualize yourself in the center with protection all around you, ready to defend and ward away anything negative floating above you that has your name on it.

Let the candles burn down halfway, and then snuff them out. Gather all the candles together in a bunch, making sure the white one remains in the middle with the piece of paper attached. Wrap the red ribbon as many times as you can around all the candles. Place the bundle somewhere where it cannot be seen, but close enough for you to feel its protective peace.

Protection Against a Specific Person

You can do this spell anytime that you want protection for yourself or your home against a specific individual. It's also great to make a protection bottle to give to a friend who is in need of protection or, by visualizing the protection they seek as you make it, to make one for your partner or your child for their own protection.

You will need:

- 1 blue candle (dress with castor oil)
- 1 red candle (dress with castor oil)

89

- 1 teaspoon of hyssop
- 1 teaspoon of mistletoe
- 1 large pinch of salt
- Mortar and pestle
- Censer
- 1 blue cloth
- 1 small, shallow white or clear plate
- 1 small blue spray bottle
- 100 mL (just under ½ cup) of distilled water
- 5 drops of rosemary oil

Method:

Light both candles, visualizing the protection you seek. Mix the hyssop and mistletoe together in a mortar and pestle until it forms into a powder. While you're doing this, say over and over again the name of the person and the protection you seek, and then blend in the salt.

Once you're finished, place the protection powder you've made in the small plate and leave it between the candles. Then burn a pinch of the powder in your censer and let the smoke engulf the room. When the smoke ends, let the candles burn down right to the end.

The following morning, pick up the remaining powder and place it in the blue spray bottle. Fill the bottle with 100 mL of distilled water and five drops of rosemary essential oil. Shake the bottle gently before covering it with a blue cloth. Leave the covered bottle out in the moonlight and sunlight for three days and three nights.

No harm will be inflicted when you use this protection spray whenever you are around the person from whom you are seeking protection. You can also do this spell for anyone else in need of protection, or make a protection spray for your home.

Protect a Stuffed Animal for Your Child

This spell is for children—either your own children or a friend's children—who are having difficulties adjusting to "lights out" or who see things in their bedroom that frighten them. These children can use this magical toy as their protector.

You will need:

- 1 orange candle (dress with baby oil)
- 1 red candle (dress with olive oil)
- 1 emerald crystal
- Censer
- 1 teaspoon of yarrow
- 1 teaspoon of basil
- 1 tablespoon of rice
- 1 stuffed animal your child likes and can identify with, such as a bear, tiger, lion, or dog

Method:

Light both candles and visualize the protection your child needs or that which scares your child. The protection needed could be from bad dreams, the bogeyman, or the kid down the street who bullies your child.

Burn the yarrow in your censer and run the smoke over the emerald crystal, then over the basil and the rice. Keep the smoke going at any cost. Now make a small incision on the stuffed animal, close to where you think its heart is, remove some of the stuffing, and place the emerald crystal, the yarrow, the basil, and the rice inside the stuffed animal's newfound heart.

Move the stuffed toy over the smoke while you say:

"Go forth and protect my child from
dreams or anything in between;
the keeper of the key to my child's safety you will be."

Then sew up the cut and say:

"Suffer not, be scared not, my child,
for this toy animal will protect you from harm."

As you're doing this, visualize the stuffed animal coming to life and sitting at the bedside of the child, with its majestic sight scaring away anyone who wishes your child harm. Leave the new keeper of your child's safety next to the candles for a while. Then give this stuffed animal to your child as a present.

Ask the child to name the new toy and to whisper its name in your ear. The new toy's name should only be known to you both, and the name used only when your child is in need and calls it out for protection.

Protection Against Someone Stealing Your Essence

This is a very powerful spell that can be used for just about any type of situation in which you feel negative energies or forces are trying to get the better of you.

You will need:

- 2 blue candles (dress with frankincense essential oil)
- 1 gold candle (dress with frankincense essential oil)
- 1 black silk square cloth
- ¼ teaspoon of dragon's blood
- 4 frankincense tears
- Small pair of scissors
- 1 teaspoon of salt
- 1 teaspoon of ague weed
- 1 meter (about three feet) of red ribbon
- 1 small pinecone

Method:

On a waning moon, preferably on a Saturday night, light the two blue candles while visualizing a blue light of protection around you. Light the gold candle and visualize gold rings, like bands of steel, that hum and repel anyone who tries to do you harm.

Spread the black cloth on your altar table, then start to burn the dragon's blood and the frankincense tears in your censer. Cut a small lock of your hair with the scissors and say: *"Lock of my hair, core of my existence."*

Gently place the lock of hair on top of the black cloth. Cut the nails of your right hand (if you are left-handed, then cut the nails of your left hand) and say:

> *"Nails, essence of my existence,*
> *secure and hold this lock and*
> *like cats' claws you will protect it*
> *and never leave it unattended."*

Place your nail clippings on top of your lock of hair, and then hold the salt in both of your hands. Rub your hands together, letting the salt fall on top of the cloth, while you say:

> *"My essences are mine and only mine*
> *And not for anyone to play or manipulate me with them."*

Now sprinkle the ague weed on top, making sure nothing spills. Make a bundle of the cloth, then tie the red ribbon around the bundle as many times as you can. As you do this, say over and over again:

> *"Curse me not with my essence,*
> *locked away they are and shall remain,*
> *never to be reached by any negative forces*
> *wanting to have them."*

Let the candles consume, and keep the black cloth in a place no one knows about but you.

Sending It Back to Negative Forces

This spell is a quick way to send back whatever has been sent to you. You are not doing a spell to pay someone back. You are simply sending back the hurt another has caused you—and feel it that person will.

You will need:

- 2 white candles (dress with olive oil)
- 1 pink candle (dress with baby oil)
- ¼ teaspoon of myrrh
- 1 teaspoon of castor oil
- 1 teaspoon of honey
- 1 teaspoon of damiana
- 1 small rubber ball
- 1 small white plate

Method:

On a Sunday when you are at peace and on your own, light the white candles with only thoughts in mind of the person who has done you harm and what that harm has done to you and your life.

Burn the myrrh in your censer to seek protection for yourself against the one who likes to inflict pain. Then mix the castor oil, the honey, and the damiana together on a small white plate. As you mix this all together, bring this person to mind and keep that thought in your mind. As you anoint the rubber ball with everything on the plate, say:

"May your own words and actions bite you back,
to never harm an innocent soul when around.
Be it for good, a lesson you will learn by
taking back your desired intent."

Hold the rubber ball in your right hand, as tight as your grip will allow. Visualize all the pain you have suffered and imagine it going inside the ball. Once you know the ball holds everything you don't want, take it to the front of the home of the one who has wished you wrong and say:

"Back to where you came from you must go
I wish no longer to play your game.
Return to the one you belong
and take with you the hurt you have caused."

Then throw the rubber ball as far as you can and you will never again play with those who don't play fair with universal games. If you don't know where this individual resides, just take the ball to the sea or a nearby creek and throw it as far as you can, and it will be express-delivered by the water element on your behalf.

To Find Who Is Doing You Wrong

You can do this spell when you know someone is out there sending you negative energies, but you don't know who it may be. This spell will aid you in identifying the source, which you can then deal with accordingly.

You will need:

- 3 drops of rosemary essential oil
- 2 drops of frankincense essential oil
- 1 red candle, 1 blue candle, 1 green candle, 1 yellow candle, and 2 white candles (dress all the candles with olive oil)
- 1 teaspoon of black pepper
- 1 map of your local area

Method:

On a Wednesday, start your oil burner and blend in both of the essential oils. Open your local map and spread it out on a table or your altar, depending on the size of the map. As you're doing this, focus on your will to find the person who is getting away with the injustice in your life. Follow this by lighting the white candles and placing them on top of the middle of the map. Say:

"Guardians of light, focus on the person I wish to find."

Light the red candle and place it on top of the map where south is, and say:

"Element of fire, be my strength and walk late at night to find the person wishing me harm."

Light the blue candle and place it on top of the map where west is and say:

"Element of water travel over sea, lakes and rivers of this town and find the person wishing me harm."

Light the yellow candle and place it on top of the map where east is and say:

"Element of air give me the intuition to know and find the person wishing me harm."

Finally, light the green candle and place it on top of the map where north is and say:

"Element of the earth, travel the hills and the plains of this town and help me find the person wishing me harm."

Sprinkle the pepper on top of the map and say:

"You, the one in the shadows
who likes to hide in the dark,
come forth and identify yourself
and let's get this masquerade out of the way."

Visualize this person coming forth and ask your guides to aid you in identifying this person behind the mask. Let the candles consume all the way to the end and leave the map out as the elements are still working on the task you have set. You will know who the person is, and then protection you shall seek.

Getting Rid of Unwanted Entities Sent to Disturb You and Your Home

To do their bidding, some negative forces seek out souls that are lost. These souls are unaware of their circumstances and quite possibly were corrupted during their physical lives. This spell will help these lost souls find light, leave your home, and continue their spiritual journeys.

You will need:

- 2 white candles (dress with olive oil)
- 1 green candle (dress with olive oil)
- 1 yellow candle (dress with olive oil)
- Censer
- A bunch of dry garlic peels
- A pinch of sulfur (make sure that you do NOT inhale the smoke; protect yourself accordingly!)
- ¼ teaspoon of dragon's blood
- 1 small bowl of water

Method:

On a Tuesday when the moon is full, light the white candles with visions of the entity you wish were out of your home. Then light the green candle and wish this entity the spiritual growth necessary to cross over. Next, light the yellow candle to bring understanding to the entity, letting it know it is time to leave you and your home alone and to go to the next stage of its spiritual journey.

Add the garlic peels on top of the charcoal tablet that is already burning in the censer. Add the dragon's blood. While the smoke circles around the candles, say:

"Go spirit of the night.
Find the light; enough is enough:
Leave us this night.
Thou shall not return, as you will find
peace on the other side."

Add the sulfur. Stand away from the smoke, and say with strength:

"Tormented you will no longer be
and no longer will you do another's dirty deeds.
Go, go, go—and get out of my home!"

Take the smoke around your home and chant the above over and over again. Start from the back of the house and finish at your front door. Repeat every day during the full moon, and again if the negative entity ever comes back to bother you.

Bringing a Partner Back

This spell can help to make a partner who has left think about you and the love you once shared. It will light a spark that will override negative forces and let in what was once real love.

You will need:

- Oil burner
- 3 drops of rose oil essential with jojoba
- 2 drops of ylang-ylang essential oil
- 2 pink candles (dress with baby oil)
- The person's astral color candle (dress with olive oil)
- Your astral color candle (dress with olive oil)
- A photograph of both of you during happy times
- ½ meter (just over 1½ feet) of pink ribbon
- 1 pinch of cinnamon powder

Method:

Mix the rose and the ylang-ylang oils in your oil burner on a Friday night, with thoughts in your mind about why your other half left. Then light the pink candles, while thinking about your love and that which you two shared and enjoyed doing together. Place the photo in the middle of the pink candles, light the person's astral color candle, and say:

> *"Think of the good times we had*
> *and the caring things said;*
> *truly search your heart*
> *and light the fire again in your heart."*

Then light your astral color candle and say:

> *"If there is still love, come back to me!*
> *If there is still trust, come back to me!*
> *If you are under a spell, think back;*
> *Open your heart and let me back inside."*

Roll the photo into the shape of a scroll and lightly tie a bow around it with the pink ribbon. Bring both astral color candles together, nearly touching, and place the photo scroll in front of them. Let it sit there until all the candles are consumed to the very end. Keep the scroll in a safe place.

Always remember that love is not to be manipulated. If it was stolen without any magic, then it wanted to be stolen! If it wasn't, the love will come back—as those types of negative spells only last for a short while. Protect your love and it will be always yours.

Not to Seek Revenge

We have no right to seek revenge no matter how sweet we may think it will be. Karma will seek it for you in other ways. But you do need to protect yourself from the infliction of negative forces.

You will need:

- 2 white candles (dress with baby oil)
- 1 black candle (dress with patchouli oil)
- 1 pink candle (dress with rose oil)
- 1 amethyst crystal
- 1 teaspoon of chamomile
- Censer and charcoal

Method:

When the moon is waxing, light both of the white candles with thoughts of peace to your soul whenever it is troubled and does not know which way to go. Burn the chamomile in your censer, and let its scent calm and purify you. Feel the peace and comfort only chamomile can bring.

Follow this by lighting the black candle. As you do, feel all the anger you have toward a specific individual or the situation that is making you want to seek revenge. Feel your anger burning away and say:

> *"Revenge feels sweet but is not for me;*
> *there are other ways to seek justice*
> *and revenge is not it."*

Light the pink candle and see anger replaced with love. Say:

> *"I am a child of the universe and*
> *a faithful member I have been.*
> *I will not tarnish it for something such as this.*
> *Revenge I will not seek*
> *but protection I seek against the ills placed upon me."*

Feel peace and understanding, the anger already a thing of the past. Seek not to harm but to receive protection. Let the candle consume, and do a protection spell or the "Sending It Back to Negative Forces" spell earlier in this chapter.

Restore the Marriage Stolen

You can do this spell if you feel your marriage or relationship with a longtime partner has come—or is coming—to an end, and you believe negative forces are part of the reason. This spell will help your partner to see the wrongs done and start fresh once again if it's meant to be.

You will need:

- Both of your astral color candles
- 1 wedding photograph (or a photo of you both together)
- 2 gold rings (it's just a symbol, so toy rings are okay)
- ½ meter (just over 1½ feet) of pink and red ribbon
- 2 teaspoons of rose water
- 1 small blue drawstring bag

- ½ teaspoon of dry yarrow
- 1 pink candle (dress with lavender essential oil)
- 1 green candle (dress with marjoram essential oil)

Method:

On a Friday night when the moon is full, place both astral color candles on top of the wedding photo. Visualize the love you had and the love you shared, which is timeless and only you could understand and bear. Look at the photo and wish yourself once again there.

Place the two gold rings in a small bowl containing the rose water. This will bring back the marriage that has been taken away.

Light the pink candle and silently ask your love if he or she feels the same way, and to search his or her heart to see if the fire still burns and to feel the love once again that was. When you light the green candle, see the love that was once there growing and never-ending, and say:

> *"Like it was before, it will be again*
> *to its original state;*

if it's mine to keep, it will be."

Let the candle consume for about ten minutes. Continue thinking of love and its return by visualizing the person to blame not wanting your partner's love anymore. While the candles are still sending your message to the universe, fold the photo as small as you can get it. Then place it inside the blue drawstring bag, adding the yarrow. Take the rings out of the rose water and wrap the red and pink ribbons around them. While you are doing this, say over and over again:

"To have and to love, from this day forward;
if under a spell it is now broken
and my love will return home shortly."

Keep the drawstring bag with you during the day and under your pillow at night.

Stay Away, My Enemy

You can do this spell when you feel all the other spells using the earlier methods have failed and enough is enough.

You will need:

- 2 blue candles (dress with marjoram essential oil)
- 1 red candle (dress with marjoram essential oil)
- 1 small glass jar
- ½ cup of vinegar
- 1 teaspoon of blue food dye
- 1 egg white
- 1 peppercorn
- 1 pinch of dry mulberry leaves
- 1 small piece of parchment paper

Method:

Light the blue candles on a Tuesday when there is no moon, and think of your enemies and the reason why you wish them to stop and be gone. Light the red candle for strength and to tell your enemies you are not as soft as they thought you were, and say:

> *"Enemy you are and enemy you will no longer be*
> *because you will no longer be able to bother me."*

Place the vinegar, the blue food dye, the egg white, the pep-percorn, and the dry mulberry leaves in the jar, and say:

> *"A bad taste in your mouth you will have*
> *when you mention my name."*

Write the name of those who want to harm you—and your wish for them to stay at arm's length—on the piece of parchment paper. Place the parchment paper inside the jar and close it. Then, with your right hand, hold the jar and shake it, making the contents go around and around. Say:

> *"Here you go around the mulberry bush,*
> *and you will keep going around until*
> *you stop harassing me for reasons I can't figure out."*

Once a day for seven days, vigorously shake the contents of the jar and say the above over and over again, and your enemy or enemies will stay away.

Chapter Nine

Spells for Self-Inflicted Curses

Banish Depression

Depression varies from person to person and is, at times, triggered by emotional upsets encountered in daily life. If you find that you lack motivation or are frequently sad or even overly irritable, you may be suffering from depression. By conducting this very simple spell, you will once again feel in control to banish depression every time you feel it coming.

You will need:

- 1 red candle
- 1 red jasper crystal (cleanse with rainwater and leave it out in the sunlight for a day)

Method:

Light the red candle as you visualize your depression being replaced by newfound inner strength, and say:

"Strength I have and inner love I have found;
depression does no longer have a place in my life."

Carry the red jasper with you at all times to fight the depression bug and always light a red candle when depressed.

Conquering Fear

Fear comes from the discomfort in situations you don't want to face. Search within and find the root of the fear that is stopping you from moving forward. Remember: fear is what you perceive it to be and not what it really is. Face the demons you carry and confront them so you don't have to deal with them again.

You will need:

- 1 wire coat hanger
- 1 letter-size (or A4-size) piece of parchment paper
- 2 clothes pegs
- 1 sink full of water mixed with 1 teaspoon of bleach

Method:

On the piece of paper, write down the fear you want to conquer and how you hope to conquer it. Then dip the paper in the sink and let it soak there for a while. Using the two clothes pegs, hang the paper on the coat hanger and leave it there to dry as you say:

"My deepest fear, out of my heart, I hang you out to dry,
once and for all out of my life."

Remove the paper from the sink. Once it is dry, burn it and take the ashes to a hill. Bury the ashes there to rest in peace.

Finding a Solution to a Problem

You will avoid daily stressors if you deal with your problems before they get out of control. Ask your guide for help and guidance for a speedy solution to your pending problem.

You will need:

- 2 white candles
- 1 bunch of white flowers
- 3 drops of lavender essential oil on your oil burner

Method:

Light both candles and place the bunch of white flowers between them. Burn lavender oil in your oil burner. Sit down and relax, thinking of your spiritual guide; he is the one that knows the troubles of your heart. In a completely meditative state, ask your guide to aid you with the problem at hand and to give you a solution that will satisfy you. You will have your answer—if not right away, then within a few days.

Gaining Self-Confidence

By gaining confidence, your mind sets out on a quest to satisfy the soul. Once accomplished, there is a newfound assurance that feeds and satisfies the soul, which will enable you to trust the decisions you make.

You will need:

- 1 red drawstring bag
- 3 acorns
- 1 teaspoon of saffron

Method:

Take the little red drawstring bag and place the three acorns and the teaspoon of saffron inside. Leave the bag out in the sunlight for three hours, and then hold it in your hand and feel the energy it now has. Feed from it to gain the confidence you wish to have.

Improve Your Lost Self-Worth

When you lose your sense of self-worth, your entire existence feels fabricated. You don't trust or believe in yourself. By building your self-worth up to where it once was, you can start to believe in and trust yourself again.

You will need:

- 1 old photograph of yourself
- 1 old piece of clothing you once wore and felt secure in
- 1 white candle (dress with sandalwood essential oil)
- 1 yellow candle (dress with sandalwood essential oil)
- 1 green candle (dress with sandalwood essential oil)

Method:

Place the photo of yourself on top of your piece of clothing and, one by one, light the candles around them both. Sit quietly and visualize the person you once were and would like to be again. Feel that energy once more; feed from the lost strength and start liking yourself. Let the candles consume right to the very end. Then place the piece of clothing and the photo under your mattress—and you will once again be filled with self-worth.

Overcome Envy

Once you are able to let go of envy, you will find that you will no longer place images of others or what they have in your mind. Be happy with what you have—it could be worse and you could have less than you do; that is true for all things physical and material.

You will need:

- 1 green candle

Method:

Light a green candle every day for seven days, always visualizing your envy burning away and leaving the core of your soul pink and full of love.

Quiet Your Nerves

We all need a time out to calm and relax the soul. Your nerves can get the better of you. By knowing how to relax, you will be able to calm your nerves.

You will need:

- 3 candles—1 pink, 1 white, 1 yellow
- 3 drops of ylang-ylang essential oil
- 4 drops of lavender essential oil
- 1 fresh white flower
- ½ cup of coconut milk
- 1 tablespoon of olive oil

Method:

Draw a warm bath and light all the candles around the bathroom. Add the oils, flower, coconut milk, and olive oil to the bath. Turn down the lights and enjoy this soothing bath—your nerves will go and you will feel as never before. You can have this bath anytime you feel the need to settle down your nerves.

Relieve Guilt

You know you have a conscience when you feel guilt and blame yourself for actions you wish you could retract. By doing the following, you will think before you act and know when not to feel guilty for actions that have been done.

You will need:

• 1 aventurine crystal (cleansed with rainwater)

Method:

Carry this crystal with you at all times; it will help you think before you act and you won't need to feel guilty for the things you've done, and for the future events to come.

Stop Overeating or Drinking

Overeating or drinking too much are signs that the physical self is not satisfied and is compensating in order to feel satisfied. Yet the feeling of satisfaction only lasts a short while—and many people find themselves overeating or drinking too much all over again. This spell will help you feel less hungry or lose the desire for more than one drink.

You will need:

- 3 almonds
- 1 teaspoon of catnip
- 1 blue drawstring bag

Method:

Place the almonds and the catnip inside the blue drawstring bag, and then hold the bag in your hand. Visualize what it is that your physical self is starving for. Carry this drawstring bag with you all the time and your hunger will no longer be for food or drink, but for life and love and whatever else your physical self craves.

To Have Mental Stability

Do this spell when you feel your mind needs stability or a rest.

You will need:

- 1 white candle
- 2 drops of rosemary essential oil
- 3 drops of sandalwood essential oil

Method:

Light the candle and burn the essential oils in your oil burner whenever your mind is in turmoil and you have a need to feel mentally stable. You can also do this spell in someone's name for their particular mental stability needs.

Improve Self-Esteem

The best way to feel good about yourself is to build your self-esteem.

You will need:

- 1 rose quartz
- 1 drop of lavender essential oil

- 1 pink candle
- 1 small pink ribbon
- 1 pink drawstring bag

Method:

After cleansing the rose quartz crystal with the lavender oil, light the pink candle and feel its loving energy, like a ball penetrating the core of your soul. Make a bow out of the pink ribbon and place both the crystal and the bow inside the pink drawstring bag. Doing so will bring love to your soul and make you feel good about who you are. It will also aid you in accomplishing the things you want to accomplish in order to bring new worth and self-esteem to your life.

Closing

$\mathcal{C}$urses are out there, and so are negative individuals, negative forces, and negative entities. They come in only if you let them, so don't let them come in. Stay mentally and physically strong. The more you acknowledge these negative forces, the more they will penetrate your spiritual and physical body for the simple reason that you are feeding them by making a big deal out of them. When you do that, you end up letting them win and achieve what they set out to do.

If you want to be treated fairly, then treat others as you wish to be treated. Don't let your ego win. If you do, you will lose the fight before it even starts. Negativity in some individuals can be contagious and hazardous to your health and spiritual growth, so try to stay away from negative people. Always try to say things in an affirmative manner. Never say "I can't." Instead, say "I can." Doing so will make achievable goals that you thought were unachievable.

Just as people can send negative thoughts, so they can send positive thoughts. If you have a dream, reach out for it and don't let anyone hold you back. No matter what they are, visualize your dreams to the universe. If you do so, you will see what can happen when you connect your positive thoughts and attitudes with the universe.

The universe and karma are always at your side, so don't worry about the wrongdoing of others. One day, justice will be achieved.

Blessed be,
Ileana

Glossary

Altar

A sacred place created for magical workings.

Astral colors

Colors of the astrological star signs.

Astral projection

Separation from the self, an out-of-body experience during which one is aware.

Aura field

The field that surrounds all of us, the colors that radiate outside our physical bodies.

Bad spirits

Earth-bound entities who have not crossed over, some of whom think they are still alive; they often do work for dark forces in return for something promised for the bad spirits' services.

Chain letter

A letter that attempts to manipulate and threaten the recipients with bad luck if the instructions in the chain letter are not followed exactly.

Chakras

The seven light points of our bodies.

Crystals

Semi-precious stones used to promote health, happiness, luck, and spirituality if carried or used with intent.

Curses

Thought patterns aimed, with destructive intent, at an individual due to the insecurities, jealousy, or anger of the one doing the curse.

Curses within

Curses people bring on themselves due to their own negative thinking.

Dark occult forces

People who practice magic obscurely and negatively.

Death card
> One of the major arcana cards of the tarot, it represents change and the death of something old that will bring something new.

Defense magic
> The form of magic used to defend ourselves from those who wish us harm.

Essential oils
> Oils extracted from flowers, plants, or resins.

Higher realm
> A higher plane of existence, a parallel universe that is not physical.

Human nature
> Behavior of people esulting from culture, attitudes, or values.

Magic
> The use of natural energies and positive visualization to create change in our lives.

Negative magic and negative workings
> The use of natural energies and negative visualization to create change in others' lives without their awareness.

Pentagram

Five-pointed star used by Wiccans and Pagans. The pentagram represents the elements and the realm between the spirit and the human body.

Perpetual curses

Curses inflicted by those who are closest to you and words and violence used to destroy a person emotionally and spiritually.

Protection

The guarding of a person and his or her loved ones against another's wrongdoings.

Unforgiven curses

Curses that continue through many different lifetimes.

Universal law

The law of karma: "What goes around, comes around."

Vampires of light

Individuals who lack self-esteem and therefore feed from yours. They leave you feeling totally exhausted though they themselves feel better when they are with you.

Index